LEARN TO DRAW... DINOSAURS!

Illustrated by Kerren Barbas Steckler
Text by Talia Levy
Designed by Heather Zschock

PETER PAUPER PRESS, INC.
White Plains, New York

For the little Stecklers

PETER PAUPER PRESS

In 1928, at the age of twenty-two, Peter Beilenson began printing books on a small press in the basement of his parents' home in Larchmont, New York. Peter—and later, his wife, Edna—sought to create fine books that sold at "prices even a pauper could afford."

Today, still family owned and operated, Peter Pauper Press continues to honor our founders' legacy of quality, value, and fun for big kids and small kids alike.

Illustrations copyright © 2015 Kerren Barbas Steckler
Designed by Heather Zschock

Copyright © 2015
Peter Pauper Press, Inc.
Manufactured for Peter Pauper Press, Inc.
202 Mamaroneck Avenue
White Plains, NY 10601
All rights reserved
ISBN 978-1-4413-1277-8
Printed in China

Published in the United Kingdom and Europe by
Peter Pauper Press, Inc., c/o White Pebble International
Unit 2, Plot 11 Terminus Road
Chichester, West Sussex PO19 8TX, UK

21 20 19 18

Visit us at www.peterpauper.com

Hey, young artists!

Are you ready to learn how to draw 22 different dinosaurs? It's easy and fun! Just follow these steps:

· ·

First, pick a dinosaur you want to draw.

Next, trace over the dinosaur with a pencil. This will give you a feel for how to draw the lines.

Then, follow the steps (shown in red) on each left-side page to draw the dinosaur on top of the basic shapes provided on each right-side page.

Lastly, if you're an awesome artist (and of course, you are!), try drawing a whole scene with one or more dinosaurs. And remember, don't worry if your drawings look different from the ones in this book—no two prehistoric creatures are exactly alike!

Along the way, check out the fun facts next to each dinosaur drawing!

GET READY! GET SET! DRAW!

To begin: Lightly draw these basic shapes.

Then: Follow each new step in red to draw this Tyrannosaurus.

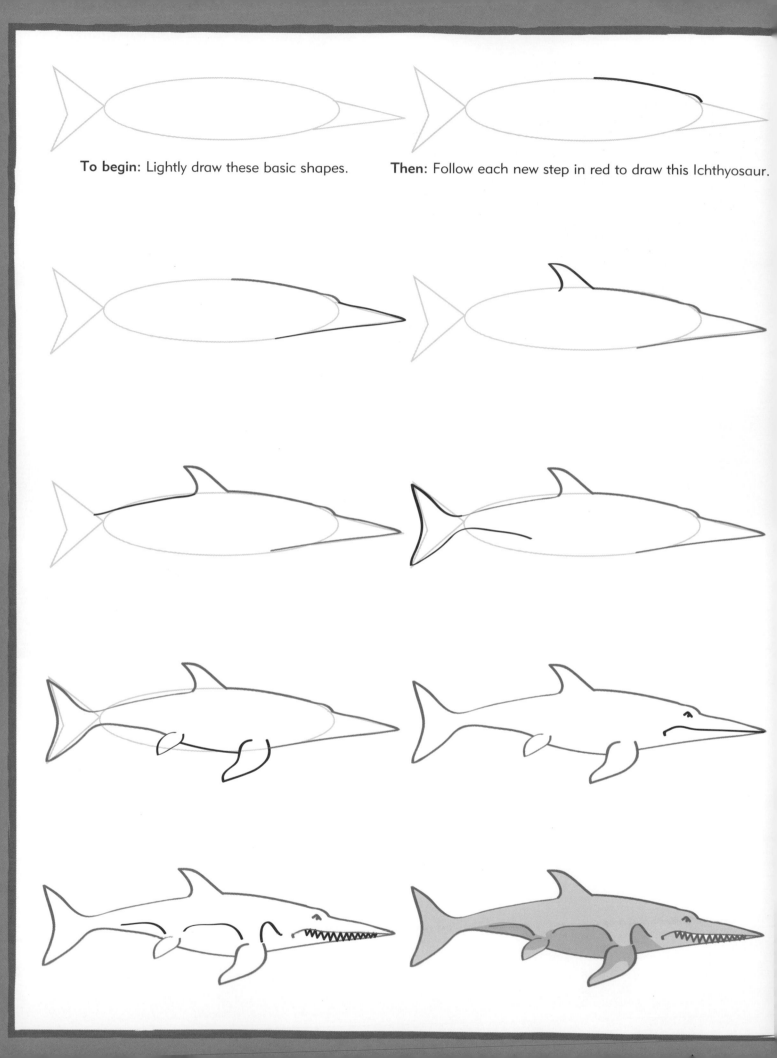

To begin: Lightly draw these basic shapes.

Then: Follow each new step in red to draw this Ichthyosaur.

ICHTHYOSAUR
(pronounced ICK-thee-oh-sore)
swam like a fish and breathed air
like a whale but was actually
a reptile, like a lizard!

First, trace over me for practice!

Then, try drawing your own
ICHTHYOSAUR over
these basic shapes!

To begin:
Lightly draw these basic shapes.

Then: Follow each new step in red to draw this Brachiosaurus.

First, trace over me for practice!

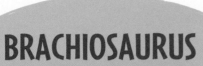used its neck to search far and wide for the roughly 440 pounds of plants it ate daily. That's some salad!

Then, try drawing your own BRACHIOSAURUS over these basic shapes!

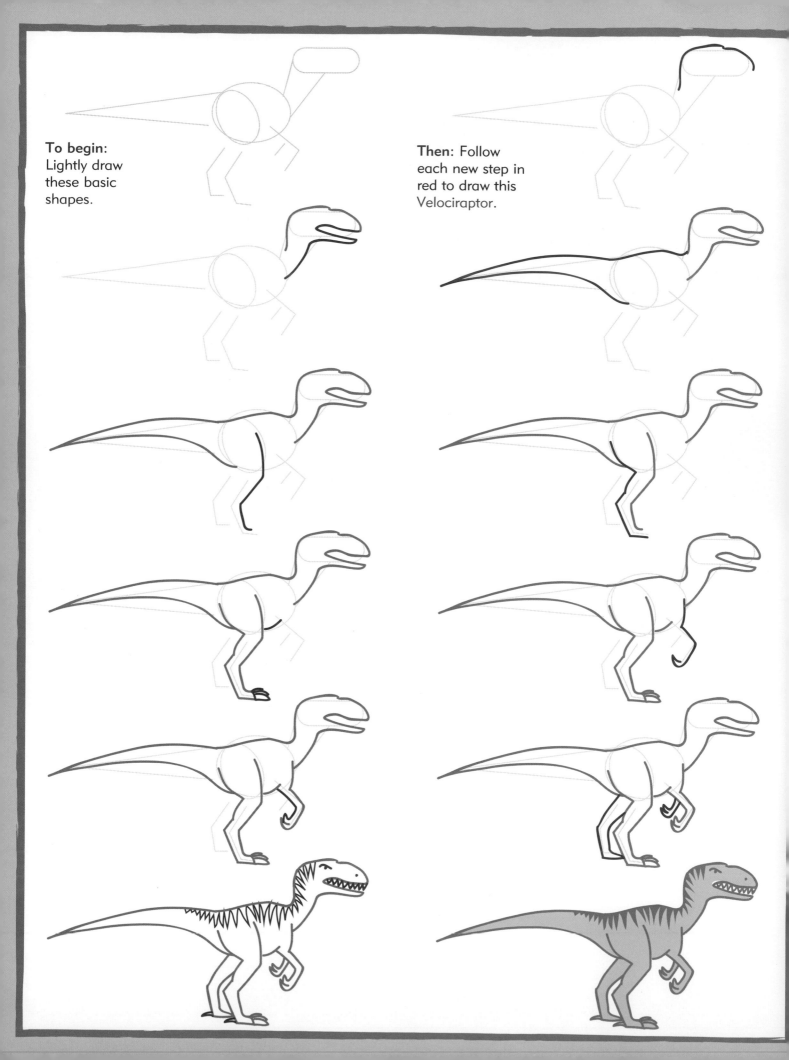

To begin: Lightly draw these basic shapes.

Then: Follow each new step in red to draw this Velociraptor.

VELOCIRAPTOR
was a miniature but mighty hunter!
It probably used the curved claws
on its feet to grip prey, as eagles
do today with their talons.

First, trace over me for practice!

Then, try drawing your own VELOCIRAPTOR over these basic shapes!

To begin: Lightly draw these basic shapes.

Then: Follow each new step in red to draw this Ankylosaurus.

To begin: Lightly draw these basic shapes.

Then: Follow each new step in red to draw this Dilophosaurus.

DILOPHOSAURUS
(pronounced die-LOAF-oh-SORE-us)
was a decorated dinosaur! It sported
a pair of half-moon-shaped bony
crests atop its head.

First, trace over me for practice!

Then, try drawing your own DILOPHOSAURUS over these basic shapes!

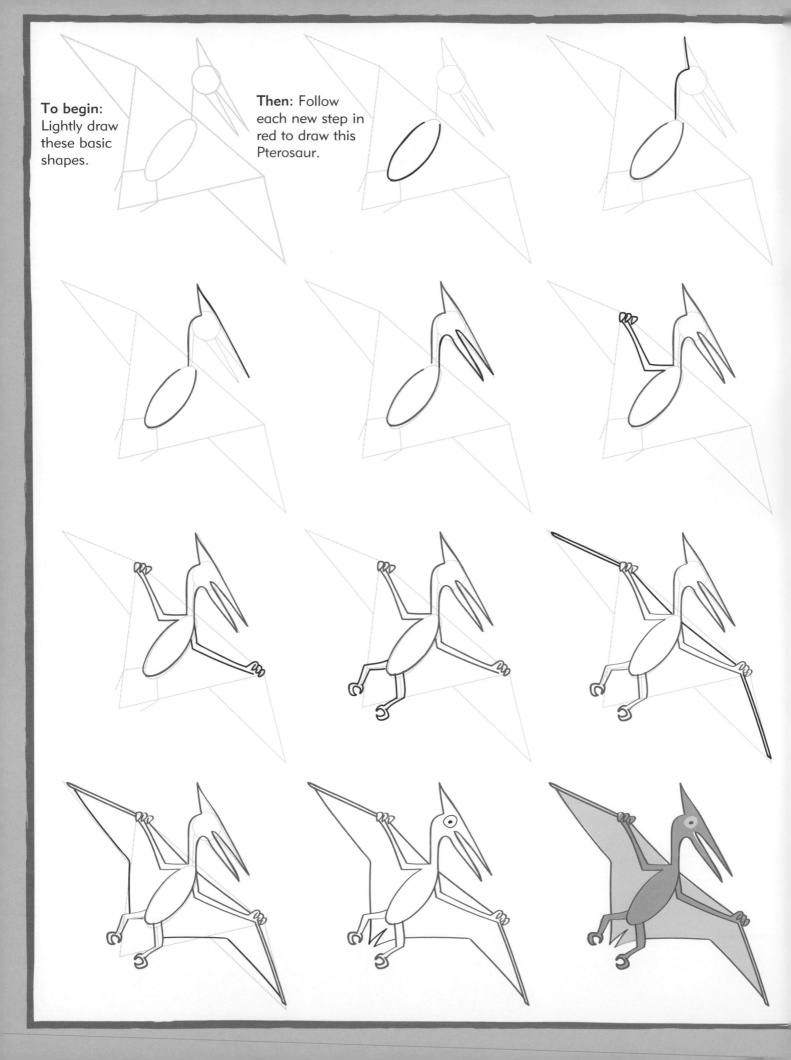

To begin: Lightly draw these basic shapes.

Then: Follow each new step in red to draw this Pterosaur.

First, trace over me for practice!

Some **PTEROSAURs** (pronounced TER-oh-sores) were the biggest creatures ever to take to the skies. A few reached the size of small planes!

Then, try drawing your own PTEROSAUR over these basic shapes!

To begin: Lightly draw these basic shapes.

Then: Follow each new step in red to draw this Allosaurus.

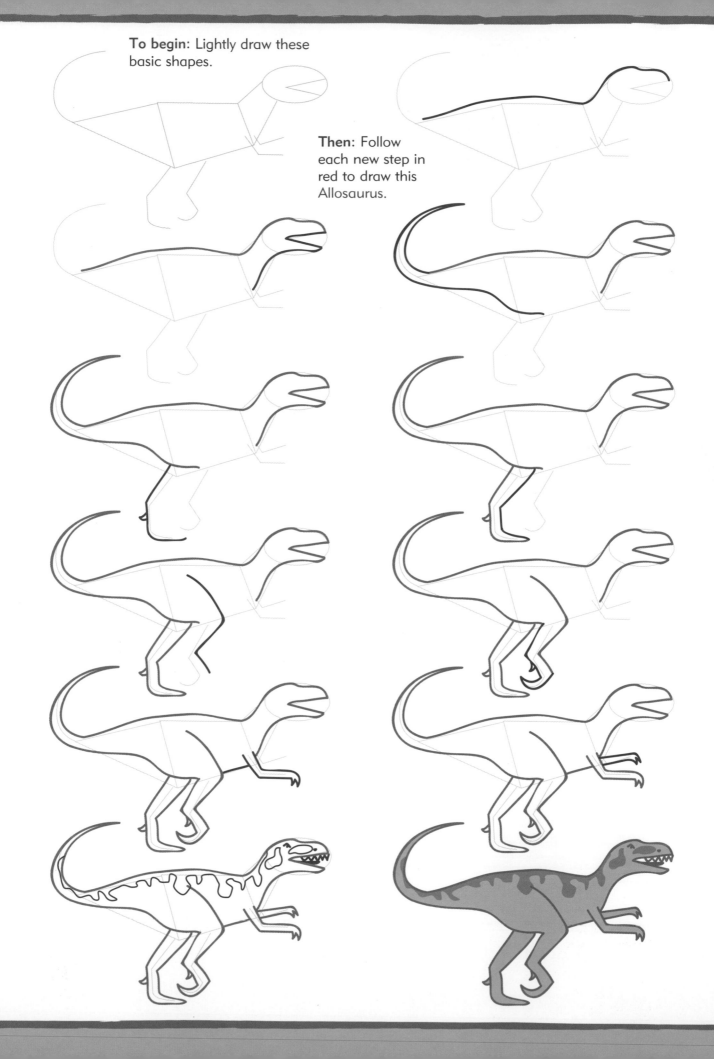

ALLOSAURUS

was as long as a school bus and made of pure muscle backed up by saw-edged teeth. Other Jurassic-period dinosaurs had to watch out!

First, trace over me for practice!

Then, try drawing your own ALLOSAURUS over these basic shapes!

To begin: Lightly draw these basic shapes.

Then: Follow each new step in red to draw this Unenlagia.

To begin: Lightly draw these basic shapes.

Then: Follow each new step in red to draw this Mosasaur.

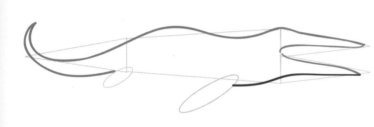

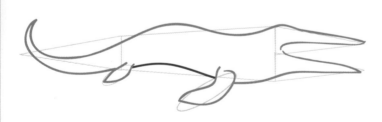

Massive **MOSASAUR** occupied the very top of the undersea food chain, preying even on sharks when it had a chance!

First, trace over me for practice!

Then, try drawing your own MOSASAUR over these basic shapes!

To begin: Lightly draw these basic shapes.

Then: Follow each new step in red to draw this Supersaurus.

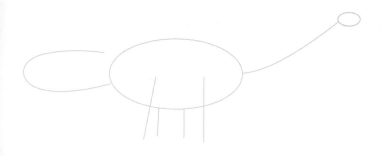
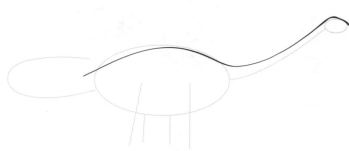

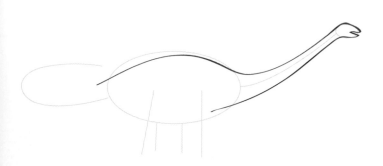
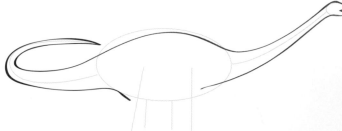

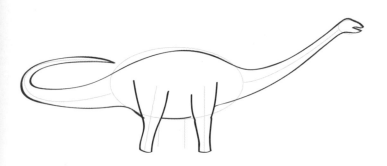
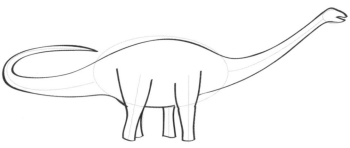

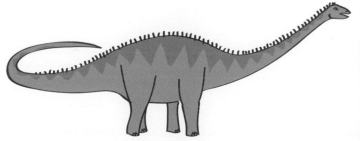

SUPERSAURUS's
super-long neck could reach the tops of trees as tall as four-story buildings!

First, trace over me for practice!

Then, try drawing your own SUPERSAURUS over these basic shapes!

To begin: Lightly draw these basic shapes.

Then: Follow each new step in red to draw this Spinosaurus.

SPINOSAURUS

may have been the biggest meat-eating dinosaur on land! It had a huge, bony "sail" sticking up from its spine.

First, trace over me for practice!

Then, try drawing your own SPINOSAURUS over these basic shapes!

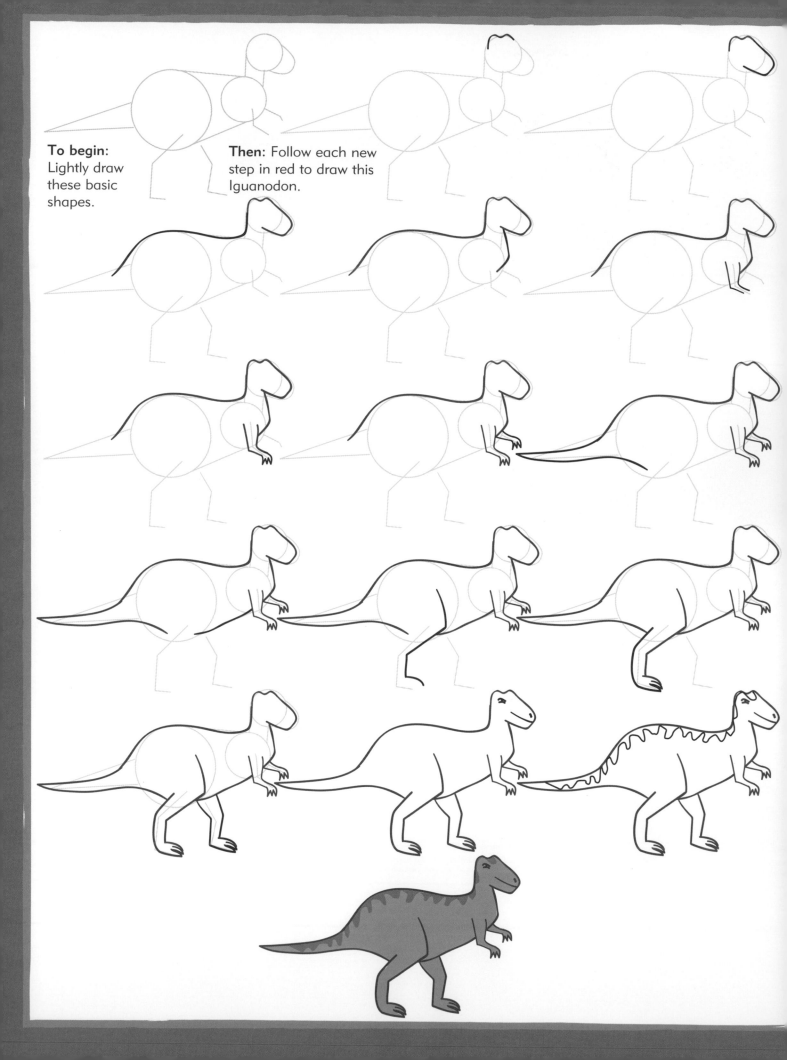

To begin: Lightly draw these basic shapes.

Then: Follow each new step in red to draw this Iguanodon.

IGUANODON
had a horned nose to help it graze on tough plants and wicked spikes on its thumbs in case of trouble!

First, trace over me for practice!

Then, try drawing your own IGUANODON over these basic shapes!

To begin: Lightly draw these basic shapes.

Then: Follow each new step in red to draw this Stegosaurus.

STEGOSAURUS's tail was equipped with four long spikes and could probably pack quite a punch when swung like a mace.

First, trace over me for practice!

Then, try drawing your own STEGOSAURUS over these basic shapes!

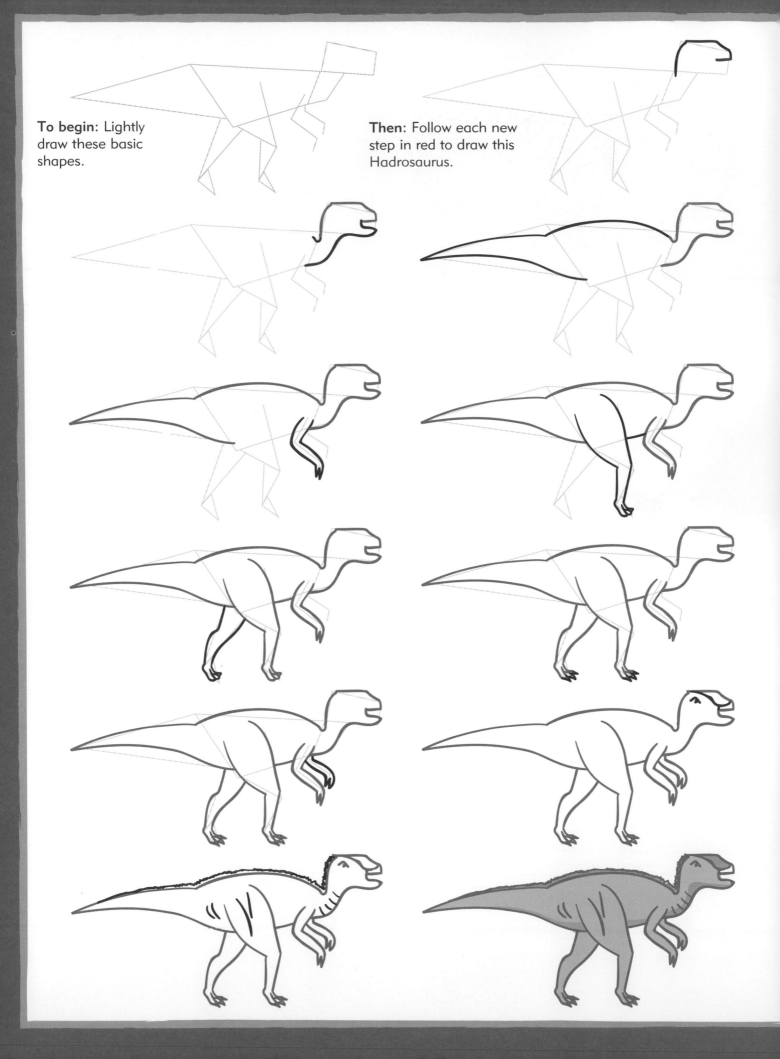

To begin: Lightly draw these basic shapes.

Then: Follow each new step in red to draw this Hadrosaurus.

Duck-billed **HADROSAURUS** had powerful flat teeth, but it only used them to grind plants.

First, trace over me for practice!

Then, try drawing your own HADROSAURUS over these basic shapes!

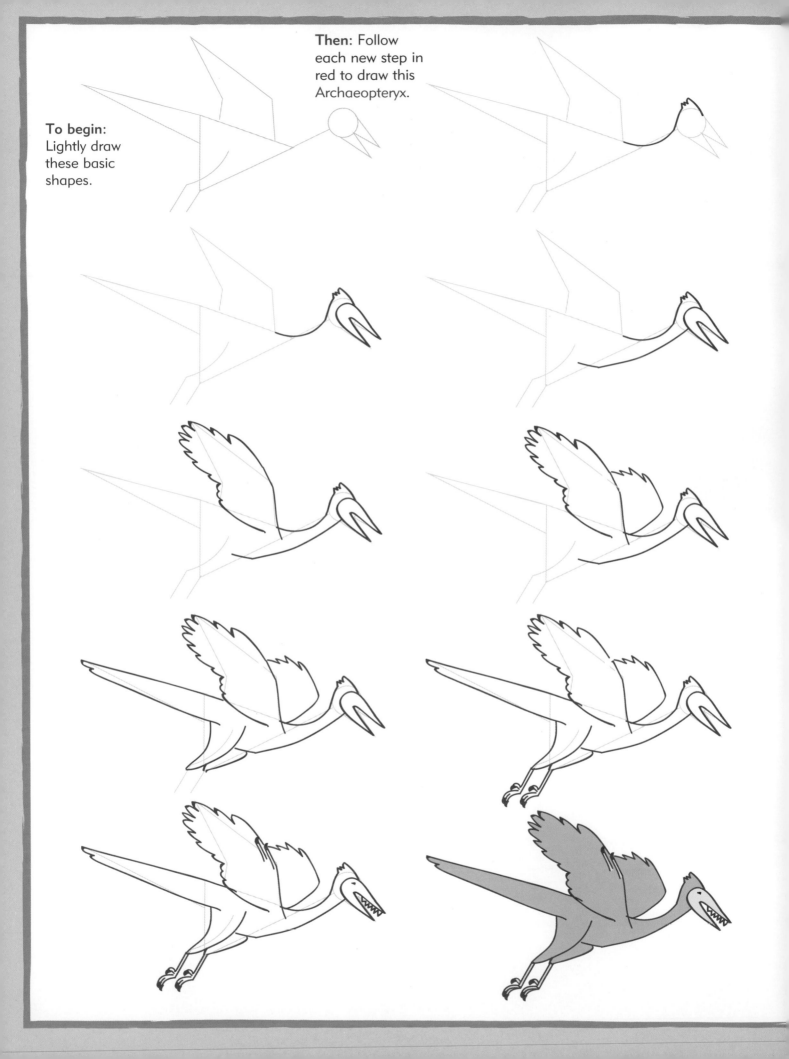

To begin: Lightly draw these basic shapes.

Then: Follow each new step in red to draw this Archaeopteryx.

To begin: Lightly draw these basic shapes.

Then: Follow each new step in red to draw this Parasaurolophus.

To begin: Lightly draw these basic shapes.

Then: Follow each new step in red to draw this Anzu.

Because of the crest on **ANZU's** head, some people jokingly called it a big chicken. But this dino was no laughing matter! Fearsome claws tipped its hands and feet.

First, trace over me for practice!

Then, try drawing your own ANZU over these basic shapes!

To begin: Lightly draw these basic shapes.

Then: Follow each new step in red to draw this Pachycephalosaurus.

PACHYCEPHALOSAURUS
(pronounced PACK-ee-sef-uh-low-SORE-us)
was a hard-headed dinosaur! It probably
used its thick skull crowned in spikes
to fight other Pachycephalosauruses.

First, trace over me for practice!

Then, try drawing your own PACHYCEPHALOSAURUS over these basic shapes!

To begin: Lightly draw these basic shapes.

Then: Follow each new step in red to draw this Therizinosaurus.

First, trace over me for practice!

THERIZINOSAURUS
(pronounced ther-iz-eye-nuh-SORE-us) wielded three giant claws on each hand. It may have had the longest claws of any animal in history!

Then, try drawing your own THERIZINOSAURUS over these basic shapes!

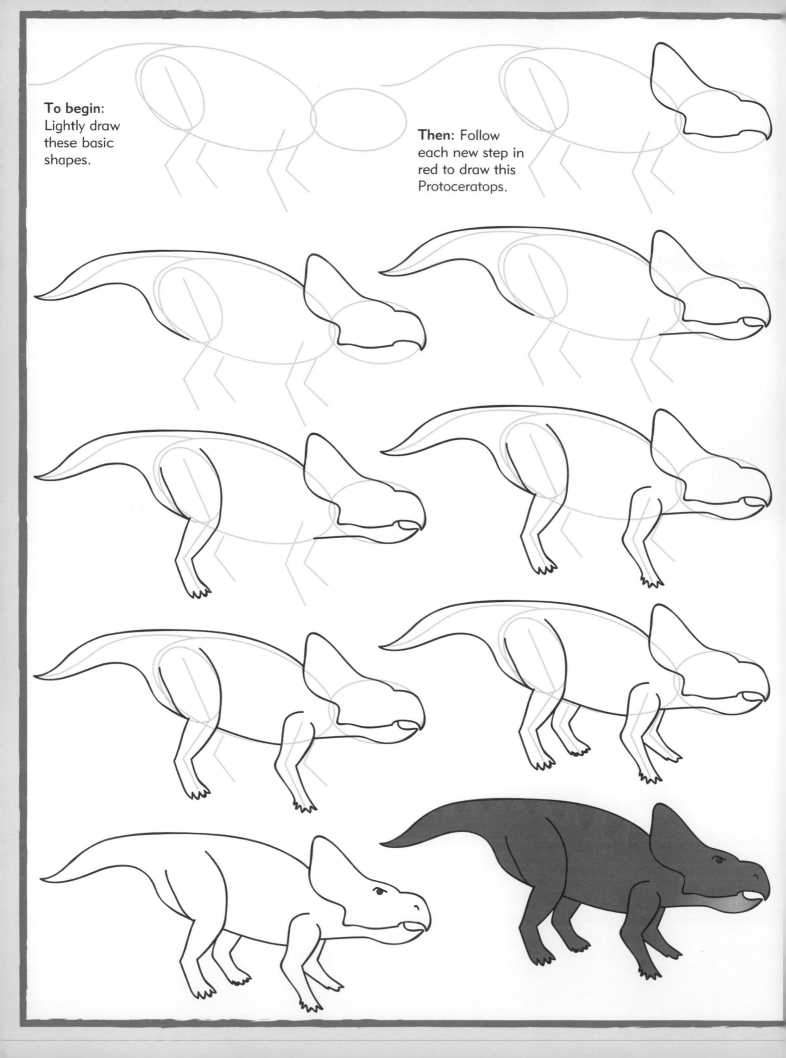

To begin: Lightly draw these basic shapes.

Then: Follow each new step in red to draw this Protoceratops.

Then, try drawing your own PROTOCERATOPS over these basic shapes!

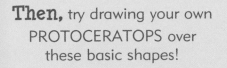

PROTOCERATOPS

(pronounced PRO-toe-SARA-tops) was a beaky little dinosaur! It grew no bigger than a small donkey, but it was cousin to the mighty Triceratops.

First, trace over me for practice!

These magnificent beasts may have vanished long ago, but they'll never truly be gone as long as people continue to study, talk about, and (naturally!) draw them. You can now visit the prehistoric world any time with the help of a pencil and some paper. What are you waiting for?

Let's rock and ROAR!